Into the Desert

Written by Mary-Anne Creasy

Illustrated by Meredith Thomas

Flying Start
to Literacy®

Contents

Preface

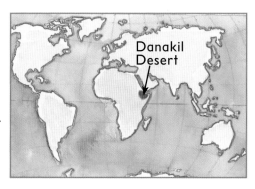

Danakil
Desert

The Danakil Desert is in
Ethiopia in Eastern Africa.
It is the hottest inhabited
place on Earth and home
to the Afar people who live in small communities. They
are nomadic and often travel from place to place, carrying
all their possessions – including their homes – with them.
They search for water, and grazing for their herds of
goats and camels.

Many Afar men also make a living carving out slabs of
salt from the salt plains that were once the seabed of
an ocean.

They get the things they cannot make themselves by
trading in nearby towns or farms. They can exchange
their livestock, butter and woven mats for items such as
flour, clothes and shoes, as well as cooking and eating
utensils and water containers.

Chapter 1

Fatuma, the daydreamer

"Don't forget to wear your shoes!" Fatuma's mother reminded her, as she went to find two long sticks.

Fatuma put her shoes on. They were uncomfortably tight, but if she did not wear them, her feet would get blisters from the hot, stony ground.

Fatuma was looking forward to a whole day herding goats, away from the village, away from her mother and the aunties who were always watching what she did.

"Aren't you ready yet, Fatuma?" said her sister, Nejat. Nejat's shawl was over her shoulders. She was wearing her shoes and had a stick in her hand.

"I'm coming," sighed Fatuma.

Mama and the aunties had gathered around to see Fatuma and Nejat off on their journey.

"Keep the goats together."

"You are going with ten goats, you come back with ten."

"Keep the sun on your back when you set out and when you come back. Don't get lost."

"You look after Nanny goat. She's the queen of the herd. And she's going to have a baby soon, so let her rest."

"Don't drink all the water at once."

Mama gave them water in the new plastic bottle that Papa had got in the town and hugged them.

"Please, do not forget you are the older one, Fatuma. Don't go off in one of your daydreams. You must look after Nejat."

"I can look after myself better than Fatuma can!" Nejat laughed.

Fatuma scowled. Mama was always telling her off. If only she didn't always daydream and get into trouble. It hadn't been a good morning for Fatuma. From the moment she opened her eyes, things had gone wrong.

* * * * *

Earlier that morning, Fatuma had woken as daylight filtered through the hut's palm frond roof. Mama lit the fire for breakfast. She fed small sticks into the flames, then set the pot of porridge over the fire. She glanced at Fatuma, who quickly shut her eyes.

"Ah, I saw your eyes open, Fatuma. Time to get up!"

Mama sighed and rubbed her back. She was going to have a baby soon, and it was getting harder for her to move around and do all the chores.

Outside, Fatuma poured water out of a plastic container into her cupped hand. She washed her face. She quickly collected more water in her hands, raced back into the hut and threw it on her sister Nejat, who was still asleep.

"Ayy!" squealed Nejat, wiping water from her face. "Mama!"

"Fatuma! Stop wasting water," cried Mama. "I'll make you collect water from the well if you do that again!"

Fatuma went back outside. She watched as two children carried a baby goat between them in a sling made out of a shawl. The goat bleated loudly as it struggled and jumped out, running to its mother.

Meanwhile, Nejat helped make the porridge.

"That's very good, Nejat," said Mama. "You have made it without lumps."

Nejat used the back of a spoon to make a hollow in the middle of the porridge, which she filled with melted spiced butter.

"Fatuma, can you please get the cups for the coffee?" said Mama.

But Fatuma didn't hear her mother's request.

"Fatuma!" Mama shook her daughter by the shoulders. "What are you doing? When are you going to stop being such a dreamer? You are the older sister, yet Nejat acts more grown up than you. Now do what I said."

"What?" said Fatuma, biting her lip. "Sorry, Mama, I didn't hear."

"Don't worry, I already have the cups, Mama," said Nejat.

Fatuma tried to make up for her behaviour. She carried the heavy pot to another hut, the one they used for eating. Inside the hut, Papa and her uncles were seated in a circle on the ground, waiting for their breakfast.

"Are you sure Fatuma and Nejat are capable of taking the goat herd out to graze?" said one of the men to Papa. "The closest grazing is two hours walk from here."

"They'll be fine, they've done it before with their mother. They know where to go. Besides, there is no one else. We have to dig for salt out in the desert today and the women are travelling to the well to get water."

"Look after the goats, Fatuma," added Papa. "They are our most valuable possession. You must concentrate. Don't slip into one of your daydreams and get lost."

The two girls sat outside the eating hut and ate their porridge. Nejat could hear the goats bleating.

"Oh no, you haven't forgotten to milk the goats, have you?" said Nejat. "Hurry, Fatuma, or we won't be able to take the goats out today."

Fatuma shook herself out of her daydream.

Mama was squatting to milk a goat. The milk squirted and frothed into a bowl.

"Sorry mother, we forgot to milk them," said Nejat.

Mama looked up at Fatuma and shook her head, pressed her lips together and said nothing.

* * * * *

As Fatuma walked, she remembered that look in Mama's eyes. It made Fatuma feel sad inside and angry with herself. She banged the stick on the ground again and ran to catch up with Nejat.

Chapter 2

A hot, sandy desert

As the sun climbed higher in the sky, the air was hot and still. The sisters walked behind the goats, waving their sticks to keep the herd together. They took turns carrying the heavy bottle of water tied onto their back.

Fatuma stared out at the rocky horizon. She imagined that the mountains in the distance were rainclouds and she tried to remember the feeling of rain on her skin. When they lived south near the river, sometimes it would rain for days and days. She, Nejat and the other children would go out and play in the sudden showers. She longed to feel the cool rain on her skin again.

Fatuma's feet were rubbing painfully in her shoes and she wished she could take them off and soothe her feet with the precious water. Nejat was shuffling her feet, making dust clouds. She dragged her stick on the ground and began singing tunelessly.

"Stop singing," said Fatuma. "You've been singing that song for weeks and I don't like it!"

But Nejat ignored her and sang louder.

"Stop!" shouted Fatuma. She quickened her pace until she was behind her sister. Fatuma reached out to grab her sister's braided hair.

A sudden gust of wind blew sand into Fatuma's face. She turned and saw an enormous cloud of sand on the horizon. The cloud was headed in their direction.

"Oh, no, Nejat. It's a sandstorm!" she shouted in alarm. "We have to find shelter. Cover your face with your shawl."

They tied their shawls around their heads and walked as fast as they could to find a place to shelter. The goats started bleating and jostling as the wind picked up.

The wind whipped up their shawls as the burning hot sand blasted into their faces. The surrounding desert disappeared into a brown haze.

"I can't see anything," cried Nejat.

The goats bleated and shrieked in alarm, then they ran, skipping over the rocky ground until they disappeared into a long, shallow crevice in the ground.

"Follow the goats!" called Fatuma. She grabbed Nejat's hand and helped her climb down into the rocky crevice. Dirt was pouring in, covering their feet.

"Quick, let's get out!" Nejat began to scramble out, but Fatuma held her arm.

"No, we're safer here," said Fatuma.

The girls sat shielding each other with their shawls, making a tent. They were able to breathe underneath this tent, the shawls filtering out the sand from the air.

"Are all the goats here?" asked Nejat. "We have to count them."

"Let's just wait until the storm is over. Then we'll count them," said Fatuma.

The girls drank some water as the wind howled above them. Then they dozed as they waited for the sandstorm to blow over.

Chapter 3

The lost goat

Fatuma woke to the sound of bleating goats scrambling out of the crevice. The sun was now high in the sky.

"Quick Nejat! The goats are getting out!"

The girls brushed off the sand and clambered up the side of the crevice. The wind had finally died down and the air was clear. The goats were calmer now and wandered about, but they kept close to the girls after their adventure.

Nejat said, "Let's count them. One, two, three, four . . ."

"Where's Nanny?" said Fatuma suddenly. They looked around frantically.

"Oh, no! Where is she?" said Nejat, her voice cracking. "We've lost her!" Her face crumpled and tears welled up in her eyes.

"It's alright, Nejat," said Fatuma. "Let's have a drink and we'll look for her. Her belly's so big she won't have gone far."

Fatuma climbed back down into the crevice and found the water bottle, but when she picked it up it felt light. She shook it. The bottle was empty. She felt the lid. It was loose. The water must have leaked out!

She clambered back out of the hole. Nejat saw her sister's face.

"What, what is it?" Nejat grabbed the water bottle. "It's all gone! You didn't put the lid on properly!" She threw it on the ground. "What are we going to do?" Nejat yelled.

Fatuma saw the fear in her sister's eyes. She knew she had to be calm and strong – she was the older one.

"I know. We'll milk one of the goats," said Fatuma.

Fatuma pulled a goat by the ear and dragged it away from the herd.

"Come on, Nejat, milk some into your hand. It's the only way."

Nejat tried, but nothing came out. The goat was too stressed, and so was Nejat.

"Fatuma, what will we do?"

"Ssh, I'm trying to think." Fatuma looked around at the rocky landscape. Which direction had they come from? The sandstorm had disoriented her and now that the sun was directly overhead and not on their backs, they were lost. Fatuma didn't know in which direction to walk, but she didn't want to tell Nejat.

As she scanned the horizon, she could see a ridge of green in the distance. This gave Fatuma an idea.

"We'll go over there, where it's green. The goats can graze and there might be water."

"But what about Nanny goat? We have to find her. Mama will be so angry if we lose her."

Nejat began to walk the other way, calling for the goat.

Fatuma ran to her sister and grabbed her arm. "Nejat, we can't look for Nanny now. We have to find water."

As they walked, Fatuma tried to remember what their mother had told her about finding water in the desert. She had taken them out herding a few weeks ago, but Fatuma hadn't been listening.

Nejat suddenly pointed at a pile of rocks balanced on top of each other.

"Look, Fatuma, there's a well!"

"There's water there? How do you know?"

"Don't you remember? Mama told us that day we went herding with her."

Quickly but carefully, they unstacked the flat rocks until they found a hollow. Inside, tied to a rock with a thin piece of rope, was a tin can. Nejat lowered it gently, then pulled it up.

Nejat took a gulp from the can, then passed it to Fatuma. The girls continued dipping the can into the well and drinking until their thirst had disappeared. They filled up the water bottle, then carefully replaced the can inside the hollow and fitted the rocks back into place.

Soon they reached the green ridge of leafy shrubs. The goats eagerly chewed the broad moist leaves on the small trees. The girls lay in the shade of the shrubs and rested.

Chapter 4

Which way is home?

"Come on, Nejat, we have to go," said Fatuma. "We have to find Nanny before it gets dark."

The sun was getting lower in the sky. Fatuma wasn't sure how long it would take them to walk home. The sandstorm and their sleep had confused her. She could not tell how long they had been away, or how far they had come.

They called the goats. They were happy to follow the girls. They had eaten well and were ready to go home. The girls walked with the burning sun on their backs. They passed the well, which hopefully meant they were going in the right direction.

They were so tired, but they had to keep going. Fatuma was worried – the sun was now low in the sky, and Mama had said to keep the sun on their backs so they would know which way to go. If the sun went down before they reached home, they might wander in the wrong direction. And in the evening, deadly scorpions came out to hunt.

"How long until we get home?" asked Nejat.

"Not long," said Fatuma.

"Are we nearly there?" asked Nejat again.

"I don't know," said Fatuma impatiently. "I mean yes, I think so." She did not want to make Nejat frightened.

Nejat stopped talking and her head drooped as they trudged along the stony ground. The goats had even stopped bleating. The silence made the hot air seem heavier.

"Listen, Nejat," said Fatuma. "Can you hear that noise?"

In the distance, there was a faint bleating sound.

"Could it be Nanny goat?" said Nejat.

"Come on!" shouted Fatuma.

Despite their tiredness, she and Nejat ran towards the sound. It was coming from the crevice where they had rested during the sandstorm.

They looked down. There was Nanny goat, standing with three newborn baby goats, nestling in the ground. Nanny looked up at them and bleated loudly.

"She must have come back here after we left," said Fatuma.

"Three babies!" said Nejat excitedly, momentarily forgetting their ordeal.

"The baby goats can't get out by themselves, we'll have to carry them," said Fatuma. "I'll get down and pass them up to you."

She climbed down into the crevice, gently picked up the baby goats and, one by one, passed them up to Nejat, who laid them on the ground.

Nanny goat bleated in alarm and immediately scampered out to her babies.

They were small and weak, so Nejat and Fatuma had to help them find Nanny's milk.

"How will we get them home?" said Nejat. "We can't carry three baby goats. What will we do?"

Fatuma closed her eyes and began to think. Then she remembered what she had seen in the village that morning.

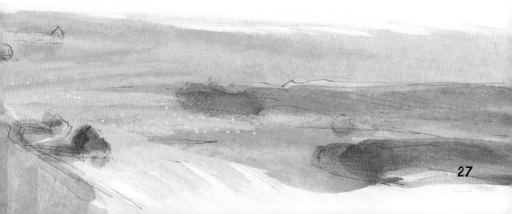

"We'll use my shawl."

Fatuma took off her shawl and tied two ends together to make a sling. Then she laid it on the ground and gently put the triplets on top. Fatuma picked up one side and Nejat took the other.

"Now, let's go," said Fatuma and they began walking, with Nanny goat bleating anxiously behind them. All the other goats followed Nanny, so the girls did not have to worry about herding them together.

Night was almost upon the desert and a small half moon shone weakly in the sky. The only sound was the goats trotting. They had drunk nearly all the water, and Fatuma's feet were raw and painful. She longed to take off her shoes now that the ground was cooler, but the scorpions would be coming out to hunt and she couldn't risk stepping on one. Would they ever reach home?

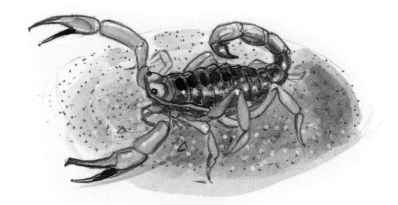

Fatuma suddenly felt frightened. "Sing your song, Nejat."

Fatuma hummed along to Nejat's song to take her mind off her fear.

Then Fatuma saw something, a dim yellow light flickering in the distance. Fatuma peered forward. Was that the village?

Fatuma heard a sound. It was their mother's voice. "Fatuma! Nejat!"

"Mama!" Fatuma tried to cry out, but her throat was so dry she could only croak.

"Mama! Mama!" Nejat screamed. "We're here!"

Then after a few minutes, out of the gloom, a shape appeared. It was their mother. She hugged them, crying, "Fatuma! Nejat!"

Their aunties came rushing towards them and hugged them, too.

"Where have you been?"

"What happened?"

"Did you get lost?"

"What are you carrying?"

"OOOH, three baby goats! Clever Nanny!"

Their mother said, "What happened out there? Why are you so late? We were so worried." She looked at Fatuma's face. "I hope you didn't get into one of your dreams again Fatuma."

"Mama, no," said Nejat firmly. "Fatuma is not a dreamer, she got us and ALL the goats home. Fatuma is a thinker!"

"Yes, you're right. You must be clever, to go out with ten goats and come back with 13!" said Mama.

A note from the author

I once watched a documentary about the people of the Danakil Desert. I learnt about their life and how they survive. They have passed down their skills and their knowledge of the environment over thousands of years. Within the tribes, children are often carers for the goats, tending to them, and taking them to find food.

Although the children would be accustomed to their environment, there could still be danger and unexpected disasters. Sometimes the children would have to cope in the desert on their own.

For this story, I tried to imagine two sisters who would fight and argue, and try to get each other into trouble just like any children do. In ordeals like this, their personality traits could affect their chances of survival. What if neither of them remembered how to find water? How could they carry three baby goats home? In the end, they survive because of Nejat's knowledge and Fatuma's dreamy character.